Eurythmy

Movements and Meditations

A *Journey to the Heart of Language*

Cynthia Hoven

with illustrations by Renée Parks

Cynthia Hoven
with illustrations by Renée Parks
Cover art by Keiko Papic
Copyright © 2012 Cynthia Hoven
All rights reserved.
ISBN: 0615631584
ISBN-13: 978-0615631585 (HeartSong Press)

For Rudolf Steiner, who first taught Eurythmy.
For Jeane Schwarzkopf, my teacher and my friend.
For Michael Leber, my steadfast mentor.
For Svava, Gena and Virginia, my readers and advisors.
And with thanks to Harald and Katrina, whose steadfast love fills my days.

Contents

Part One

Part Two

Making Language Visible

v

What does my Creator, working out of primeval, cosmic being, do in me as a human being? If you would give an answer to this question you must make Eurythmy movements. God eurythmises, and as the result of His Eurythmy there arises the human form.

Rudolf Steiner, <u>Eurythmy as Visible Speech,</u> p. 37

Anastas Ltd.,The Throne, Weobley Herfordshire HR4 85W.

The world speaks. Above all, it says the speaking itself. Or does the speaking say the World?

Georg Kühlewind, <u>Das Gewahrwerden des Logos,</u> p. 19

Verlag Freies Geisterleben, Stuttgart, Germany

The Dance

Consciousness expresses itself through creation. The world we live in is the dance of the creator. Dancers come and go in the twinkling of an eye. But the dance lives on. On many an occasion when I am dancing, I have felt touched by something sacred. In those moments, I felt my spirit soar and become one with everything that exists.

I become the stars and the moon. I become the lover and the beloved. I become the victor and the vanquished. I become that master and the slave. I become the singer and the song. I become the knower and the known. I keep on dancing…Then it is the eternal dance of creation. The creator and the creation merge into one wholeness of joy. I keep on dancing…and dancing…and dancing. Until there is only…the dance.

Michael Jackson, the Dangerous album

Part One

The Art of Em-bodying the Word

My Journey to Eurythmy

Eurythmy. The word is smooth in the mouth, fluid to the ear. To the Greeks, it means "harmonious rhythm."

In Eurythmy, we dance with the forces of creation. Rudolf Steiner (1861–1925) first spoke of this new art form in 1911, when he was asked what manner of dance might be appropriate for this age. He responded to the question by creating a new art of movement that develops entirely out of the experience of the spiritual-physical nature of the human being. In Eurythmy, the self-aware soul speaks and sings through articulate gestures that transpose language and music into dance.

I find that the essential spiritual flame that lives in each human being becomes revealed when we do Eurythmy. No matter the body size, no matter the talent, every person can connect with the warmth and light of their inner heart through this expressive art. This is the great and sacred joy that I have been privileged to experience again and again over the years, as I have taught the foundations of this art to literally thousands of people.

I began my Eurythmy journey when I was 23. After earning my college degrees in general sciences and psychology, I bought a one-way ticket to Europe and began a two-year pilgrimage around the world. My youthful hope was to find a spiritual teacher, and I thought the best place to seek would be India. When I did not find what I was looking for there, I continued my journey to the Far East, through lands that were far off the beaten track, including Vietnam during the end of the war years. My journey culminated with a year in Japan, where I studied with a man who was a Shinto priest, kundalini yoga master, an acupuncturist, and a parapsychologist. Even my work with him, however, did not lead me to the living spiritual experience I was seeking. I was left with a vague despondency, asking myself how I could find a path of spiritual inquiry relevant for the modern western soul.

I returned to the United States in 1974, sensing that it was time to find my future there. Having traveled through so many distant lands and cultures, I decided to move to California, hoping that amongst all the new and innovative endeavors that were thriving there, I would find my own next step.

A period of restless seeking followed, in which I became increasingly aware of my deep longing to explore the depths of spiritual knowledge. I could remember that even as a child, I had set myself the goal of finding a life task that would "combine science and religion." I was clear that I wanted to find a path that would support clear consciousness and not ask of me to submit to an external authority, be it to a dogma or to a spiritual guru. I had, moreover, already excelled in the sciences in college, and knew that a purely scientific pursuit for me would be one-sided. Thus I began to look for what I called "a spiritual art form that could serve to heal people."

It was surely destiny that led me to Eurythmy. On New Year's morning in 1975, a friend told me of two women who had just returned from Switzerland to their native California and were prepared to offer the first Eurythmy training on the west coast of North America. I had never heard of Eurythmy nor had I ever considered that the healing art form I was seeking might be a movement art, but when I heard of this work, I was intrigued. I learned that Eurythmy is a relatively new art, envisioned and articulated by Dr. Rudolf Steiner, who had been active as a spiritual, scientific and cultural leader in Europe at the beginning of the 20th century. I was told of the living body of knowledge he created, known as Anthroposophy, and of his method of inquiry into relationships between the spiritual and physical worlds, known as *spiritual science*. I learned that Rudolf Steiner is perhaps best known as the founder of Waldorf education and bio-dynamic agriculture, but his legacy can be found in architecture, sculpture, religious and cultural studies, medicine and pharmacology, economics and many other fields.

That week I experienced my first Eurythmy class. I was invited to imagine the seed of a plant living in my soul, and to curve my arms and my hands to my chest to contract my energy around it. Then I was to imagine the forces of life stirring in the seed, and to feel it wanting to grow, downwards through roots, and upward through stem and leaves and flowers. As I followed this mental imagination with my energy, I felt myself become grounded in my feet and weightless in the arms. I allowed my arms to unfold like leaves and be lifted to the heights. I discovered that my mental pictures could actually become real experiences in my body.

What was this? How could my inner activity affect my relationship to gravity in this way? How could I feel both so light and so grounded? I discovered that in Eurythmy I would learn to play artistically with the way that I live in my body and in my soul. To me this was more interesting than yoga or sitting meditation practices. This was a way of learning to be inwardly creative, spiritually attuned, and expressive in my gestures.

I was inspired enough to want to explore where this path might lead me. Thus it was that I embarked on a four-year full-time training at the Goldridge Eurythmy School in Auburn, California.

Student Years

We were a small class of six people in the beginning of my training, three men and three women. Our first lessons led us into an exploration of how we stand, walk and move. I learned to develop a new awareness of how my feet meet the earth and how they serve me when I walk. I became aware of my posture, and how to carry the light of heaven and the strength of gravity in my upright bearing. I came to feel my arms and how they move, and understood that I could learn to develop every gesture to be a powerful expression of my inmost self. I learned to open my heart and let it be my source of strength and honesty in my movements.

In every lesson, we also concentrated on learning to connect with one another and work as a harmonious group. As a result of our common effort, the atmosphere in the room became tangibly alive. We developed the ability to move together as organically as a flock of birds through the air or a school of fish through the water. We developed the ability to be sensitive to each other's will and intention, so that we could support one another's movements. And in a fascinating way, all the challenges of group dynamics (including qualities such as cooperation, collaboration, aggression, ambition, introversion, manipulation, evasiveness) became evident as we tried to perceive and support one another's movements. Likewise, the solutions for the challenges revealed themselves through movement as we worked through them.

Living Anthroposophy: What am I as a Human Being?

Through my experiences in Eurythmy, I came to understand what Dr. Steiner calls the "four-fold human being," for these are the tools of our art. He calls the physical body "that which remains behind in the natural world when we die." My physical body is my densest energy. Through it, I experience gravity, limitations, the directions of space, and volume. I must learn to penetrate it so I can move with my body accurately and expressively.

Rudolf Steiner calls the "etheric"–or life–body "that which keeps us alive as long as we are alive." It is that system of forces that holds our entire physical constitution integrated into an organic whole, an organism. It is a living system in constant movement, in structured and dynamic flow. In the natural world, the plants are perfect manifestations of the etheric body, as they are lifted beyond gravity to unfold in the realm of life and light. In Eurythmy, I have learned to work artistically with the life body. This means that I have learned to play with time, creating movements that unfold with liquid grace. I have learned to play with anti-gravity, so I can engage my limbs with light agility. I have learned to play with holistic fields, so the movements of hands and feet, back and belly and head are all integrated into an artistic organism.

The "astral" body is the body of sentience: we bear this in common with the animals. Through the astral body my inner soul experiences what is within me and around me. Through it, I know the colors, textures, dynamics, and movements of the world. Through it, too, I think and I feel and I will. The astral body carries the wisdom of the universe, right into my inner core and from it out again into the world. As an artist, I learn to play with how the *qualities* live as color and dynamic in my soul, and I learn to artistically evoke the qualities I need to express, as a painter chooses his palette or a musician her notes.

My "ego" or "I-Am" consciousness is the most interior part of my being. It burns as a flame in my heart, ablaze with the inexhaustible fuel of pure spirit. Through the activity of the I-am, I know myself to be a child of God. I become actively creative in my own biography. I become aware of my own motives and my intentions. I can also become the author of entirely new intentions.

Through my spiritual path, I learn to know that through the I-Am in me I can meet the I-Am of the world. This is the self-aware spirit consciousness of the universe. Through the I-Am, I engage an even deeper level of my being in Eurythmy. I become the author of my intention, becoming aware of my choice to create with my soul qualities, use my organic life field, move my physical body to express meaning.

In the course of my Eurythmy training, I learned to penetrate all of these bodies and their interactions. I worked tirelessly towards agility of the body, grace of the etheric, the capacity to create quality, and the ability to be authentic in my expression. In my Eurythmy training, I learned to become utterly open, vulnerable and real.

The Essence of Eurythmy: Visible Song and Visible Speech

In the Eurythmy training, half of the curriculum is done to the accompaniment of live music. What a joy it is to work with the compositions of Bach, Beethoven or Schumann! From the first weeks of the training, we were able to move to the creations of greater and lesser composers. As we entered into their music, we learned to feel how their dreams and thoughts unfolded into the beat, rhythm and pitch—the melodic lines and harmonies of their pieces. We were taught a way of moving that is different from what we normally understand as dance. We did not dance *to* the music, but rather learned to *become* the music. Far more: as I listened to the music, it literally became the impulse of my own will. I learned how beat lives in my bones, rhythm in my breath, pitch in my gravity and levity. I learned that my own expressions of softness or willfulness are the outpourings of musical dynamics, and that melody lines themselves are woven out of spirit realms.

Yet when Rudolf Steiner first developed Eurythmy, he promised an art form that would work primarily not with music, but with language. He perceived that, hidden behind the interplay of vowel and consonant—of rhythm, grammar and cadence—there is the power of what is called the Creative Word, The Logos.

Many ancient legends, mythologies and religious teachings tell of the world being spoken or sung into existence. The well-known prologue to the Gospel of St. John in the New Testament reads:

"In the Beginning was the Word,
and the Word was with God,
and the Word was God.
All things were made by Him,
 and without Him was not anything made that was
made."

Even as a young person, I had puzzled over these lines. I had asked myself: Shouldn't that read, "In the beginning was 'thought'?" Or "power"? What is "Word" that it could make things? Finally, in the lessons in Eurythmy, I began to understand what the true nature of the Word is. I began to experience it as the living, dynamic, meaning-filled creative source of the universe. And as we immersed ourselves in the Word, we entered the world of story and poetry and learned to let them become visible in our choreography and gesture. The art we pursued became synonymous with our spiritual path. And so, as I have drawn near to the Word, I have also drawn nearer to my Creator, and nearer to my own self. This is the substance of this book, and what I hope to share with you.

Art, Therapy and Teaching

After receiving my diploma in 1979, I joined the Goetheanum Stage Group in Dornach, Switzerland for eighteen months as an apprentice artist. There I was privileged to work on one of the largest and most beautiful stages in Europe, performing great pieces of music and poetry in Eurythmy. The first major piece I participated in was *Spring*, from the *Four Seasons* by Vivaldi. We moved to the music of a full, live chamber orchestra, and each Eurythmist made visible the melody line of a single instrumentalist. In the months that followed, I performed group and solo pieces in poetry, drama, fairy tales and music.

In the fall of 1980, I moved to Stuttgart, Germany, to begin a two-year training in Eurythmy Therapy. After having traded the scientific work of my university studies for an artistic journey, I found a deep joy in this work, in which my two loves were wedded. Here I studied anatomy, biology and physiology from doctors and therapists who had a deep appreciation for the artistic process. I learned how to apply the understanding of Eurythmy, music and language to work with a wide variety of patients. Upon completion of my training, I worked in as many hospitals and clinics in Germany and Switzerland as possible, apprenticing myself to master teachers in preparation for my eventual return to North America,

Finally, in 1983, I began the next chapter of my life, in California. I have been active in Eurythmy here ever since, performing and creating productions, doing therapeutic work with individual clients, and teaching thousands of adults. In 2002 I founded a Eurythmy training at Rudolf Steiner College in California which I led and directed for eight years.

Finding my Writer's Voice

This book has been in the process of being born for many years. Again and again, students have asked me where they can read about Eurythmy, and I have not known of books that I could recommend to them that would reveal the deep spiritual roots of our work. I, too, tried my hand at writing, but I was reluctant to create an intellectual or theoretical text about an art which I love so deeply. I thus struggled for many years to find my writer's voice.

One day a student asked me the leading question: "What do you *really* do when you do a sound in Eurythmy?" The quality of her question made me realize that she wanted me to answer the question as deeply as I could. And as I began to describe my process, I could finally envision the book that I would write.

I have learned to experience every sound in language as a spiritual being. To do a pure sound gesture in Eurythmy, I first become deeply centered and remember *who* the sound is. Making myself quiet and empty, I invoke the presence of that being, so that a greater will can suffuse my personal will. I bring in the great power and wisdom of the sound, and let its movements engage my limbs. When I do Eurythmy, I dance with the spiritual beings.

This book is thus a celebration of the beings whom I love deeply: the sounds of language. I wish to introduce the reader to each of these beings through vivid and meditative texts. My descriptions can of course not be exhaustive, for just as each person knows another in an individual way, these great beings will have introduced themselves to other Eurythmists in ways

7

different than they have to me. Nonetheless, my dance with them has been a long, dear and intimate one, and I hope to serve them well as I describe them to you.

My story will begin with the greatest story ever told: how the world was born, how we became lost from our Creator, and how we will, at length, arise as those who, out of their divine freedom, choose love.

Prologue:
Dancing the World into Being

Prologue

In the beginning was the Word.
Before the beginning was Silence.
The Creator was.
And then, the first beginning.
The Creator spoke, and all that was contained within was
poured outwards.

The Word created all that is
All that was
All that will be:
Time, space, and all beings.
The Word is the love and will of the Creator,
And contains all wisdom,
All movement.
All shapes and forms.

The Word created warmth and light and air and water,
And created our earth,
Its mountains and trees, rivers and oceans, air and sunlight, fire
and flame.

And in the fullness of time the Word became flesh.
The Word took on human form, and we became the Word.
And we are living in the great mystery of learning to speak the
Word as we grow into earthly/cosmic maturity.

In the beginning, human beings were mute.
We could not speak, but we could dance.
Even as plants dance in the wind,
As jellyfish dance in the water,
As cilia dance in our bellies,
We participated in the first dance of the creation.
Our limbs were long and loose and lithe,
And we were one with all of nature.

The dance of our bodies has become small,
but we have learned to dance with our words.
With our speech we can now name the birds and the beasts
and the butterflies,
The wind and the rain,
Thunder and lightning,
Stars and sun.
The great creative mysteries of the Word now live in our
throats,
And we can tell each other stories through our words.

Now is the time for dance to be reborn.
When we silence our voices and open our ears and hearts to
the movements behind the sounds,
We can discover the dance of the spirit Word.
Eurythmy is the name of the new dance,
The dance of the living word.

Cynthia Hoven

The Cosmic Creative Word

Dancing the World into Being

In the beginning, the primal will of creation surged forth from the first source as the speech of the Creative Word. Into the warmth of world will, unimaginably lofty spiritual beings poured forth their wisdom and light, and their activity gave rise to the widths and depths of time and space. The gods of creation danced, and out of their weaving, flowing, sculptural movements, all the shapes, forms and textures of the universe came into being.

At one time, in the deep mythological past of the earth, we as humanity could experience the gods walking in our midst and in the heavenly bodies above us. In those times we knew that we moved with the creator spirits and nature spirits. Their joy, their songs, their anger were echoed in our environment and in our souls. We danced with them and for them, praising them, appeasing them, and invoking their blessings.

In our time, however, we have forgotten the ancient dances. The world, which previously had been alive and infinitely malleable, is now dense and hard. We are intoxicated by the overwhelming power of the senses, and we no longer sense the gods shining through them.

Humanity's Journey through Matter to Freedom

It is said that humanity needed to become deeply entangled in the sense world in order to become free. So long as we walked with the gods, we could make no other choice than to obey their infinitely greater will. When, however, we became wrapped in the delights of the sense world, we became separated from our primal source, lost in egoistic self-consciousness.

Our evolution through separation, desire and egotism unfolds in our passage through the world of matter. It will eventually lead through intellectual maturity and on to spiritual self-knowledge and cosmic consciousness. In this, the material world, we can choose to live out of egotism or out of love. This is our heritage, our promise and our hope.

The physical world in which we live is too dense for higher spiritual beings to exist in their pure form. Their emissaries, the elemental beings, are enchanted into this world of substance. As long as our consciousness is superficial, we see only the world of appearances. This, the world of "maya," is the state of being specific to our current phase of evolution: this is the eye of the needle through which we must pass.

As we evolve to spiritual maturity, however, we will discover that it is possible to apprehend the spiritual world right here, through beholding the sense world with spiritual vision. We will then see that the Creative Logos, the World Word, has united Itself with the earth and with humanity. The Logos can be found in the macrocosm around us and in the microcosm within us.

The Dance and the Word

I understand the Creative Word to be the *outpouring of loving, wisdom-filled formative movements from the very heart of the Creator.* The creative spirits of the universe were dancing with the movements of the Creative Word long before we became speaking beings.

Rudolf Steiner tells a story of the birth of human speech. He tells us to imagine a scene from ancient days, long, long ago.

> We are in a forest, near a mighty tree. The sun has just risen in the east. The palmlike tree, from around which the other trees have been removed, casts mighty shadows....A priestess "sings," and her tones have in them something mighty, powerful. Those around her move in rhythmic dances. For this was one way in which "soul" entered into mankind. The mysterious rhythms which one had heard from Nature were imitated by the movements of the limbs. One thereby felt *at one* with nature and with the powers acting in her.[1]

Through this story we are reminded that human beings have been dancing since the beginning of time. We may imagine that we once lived in much closer harmony with nature, and that through dancing we had an immediate and

---

[1]   Rudolf Steiner. *Cosmic Memory: Prehistory of Earth and Man.* New York: Harper and Row, 1959, p. 82

intimate conversation with the creative spirits we could feel all around us. Their wisdom-filled movements permeated the air and water around us, bending and curving, flowing and sculpting the shapes of natural things. The dynamic pulsing of their gestures inspired our dances, as we imitated them and allowed them to instruct and carry us. Rudolf Steiner suggests that in those most ancient days, we were not yet capable of speech. We dreamed into the world and yet our larynxes were not yet able to speak of it.

Over the course of long ages of time, the contours of the world have become much more defined, and our bodies more solid and defined. Now, in our present, intellectual age, we are largely restricted to the confines of our physical bodies, unaware of the life forces that surge through us and weave through our bodies as a holistic system. Our limbs are more closely bound to gravity, and our dances more earth-bound.

However, in place of the first dance, we have received a great gift: we have learned to dance with our words. We now have voices that can give names to things and speak about the world. Instead of dancing with our limbs, we can now employ the marvelous instruments of mouth, tongue and larynx to make incredibly fine movements that cause the air to sparkle, ripple and soar. Now with our speech—no longer with our limbs—we imitate the first dance of the gods, and communicate the essence of our inner life to one another. The great creative mysteries of the Word have now entered into the human being. The original Eurythmy has become Language.

The movements that live within language are the same movements that sculpted the worlds around and within us. As witnesses of Creation, we discover and give true names to things and ideas.

Language is a riotous dance of sounds, and each sound has movement, gesture and color. Each sound is a spiritual being, godlike in attributes and serving the great Logos being, the World Word. Through the cooperative interplay of their wisdom and movement, the building blocks of the world are laid. As we learn to live into the movements of the sounds, we resurrect the dance of creation.

Eurythmy: the New Dance of the Word

The entirety of the manifest world was "spoken" into existence through the pre-verbal "dance." This Word-Dance penetrates every aspect of our being, of our universe.

Yet through the long ages of evolution, we increasingly identified with our physical existence. This has affected all aspects of our being, including our language and our dance. The original Word of Creation has "died" into matter.

Nonetheless, whenever we speak, we create movement patterns in the etheric or life-space that surrounds us. In the art of Eurythmy, Rudolf Steiner was able to teach us how to read these movements in space, and how to transpose them into movements of the whole body. Thus, the movements of Eurythmy grow beyond the temporal and embody divine archetypal forces. Eurythmy is an utterly modern art form that moves with the power of the speech and dance of the gods of long ago.

Eurythmy is the dance reborn, the dance of the new word. As a Eurythmist, I have been led in a new and unexpected way to the gods and goddesses of the sounds, who as great spirit beings have made the entire world. As I dance with them, I come to know them as beings of force and wisdom and color. I learn to recognize the great sculptors of the universe, they who have made heaven and earth. I discover that they have given themselves unto us entirely, shaping our bodies and weaving the weft of our thoughts and our souls.

This dance is dynamically, powerfully *alive,* for it exists in the holistic field that surrounds and upholds living systems on the earth. In Eurythmy, I use my body not merely as an instrument of physical dance: I move the entire space around me. I perceive it, engage it, color it and shape it. My awareness extends beyond the confines of the room I move in. I work with lines, planes and spheres of space, and experience these alive and responding to me. I experience levity, the sun-forces that draw plant life upwards. Above all, I pour into my movements the same consciousness and meaning that I employ when I speak, causing them to resound with inaudible sound.

Thus in Eurythmy, I experience the deepest mystery of all: myself as a microcosm, and all the forces of creation that lie within me, seeds for a new creation. When I am truly graced, I can experience that the space in which I do Eurythmy is suffused with the pure substance of love.

We stand now at the point when new spiritual capacities can unfold within us. Through our emerging consciousness, the creative Logos will become self-aware in us. We will know ourselves to be the bearers of the World Word, and we will be generators of the new meaning of the earth. Through these new capacities, we ourselves become the Logos, the creative Word of creation. In Eurythmy, the gods of creation dance with us on the earth.

Eurythmy as "Visible Speech"

Vowels and Consonants

Imagine the creation of the earth. Picture divine hands shaping the mountains, valleys and plains, the birds and the beasts and the plants, with infinitely powerful and fine, delicate movements. Feel how some gestures are round and voluptuous, while others are sharp or pointed.

Anticipate then how these gestures live again in magnificent but greatly compacted forms in our human language.

The manifestation of these formative forces are found in language in our *consonants*, which are shaped by palate, tongue, teeth and lips with explosive, liquid, round or sibilant gesture. We use these sparkling sounds to describe mountains and rivers and stars. We use them to give names to all the plants and all the animals of our world.

The sculptural forces that we find in the consonants have likewise formed the shape of our body, the temple for our spirit. The same will and wisdom and movement found in the universe around us live within us as well.

> When we speak the *consonants* or move them in
> Eurythmy, we dance with the sculptural forces that
> shaped creation.

When the breath of spirit was breathed into the human being, we became ensouled, bearers of an inner life which reflects the whole of the universe outside. We became self-aware, and authors of our destiny. The manifold ways we experience self and world are experienced in the "singing sounds," the *vowels*. Through these the soul speaks back to the world.

The inner life of human beings comes to expression in language in the vowels. They express our joy, our sorrow, our love, our power.

When we speak the *vowels* or move them in
Eurythmy, we express the soul's relationship to the
world.

From Sounds to Words

The essays in this book offer an experience of the deeper meaning of individual sounds. Sounds alone, however, are only the doorway to meaning. When we speak, we make use of virtually limitless combinations of sounds to make words.

In words, vowels and consonants interact in lively combinations. The consonants describe how the shapes and movements of an object are experienced: the vowels express how the soul responds to the object or experience.

As a Eurythmist, I must deepen myself into the inner core of the words. I must play with the words so creatively that their inner nature reveals itself. The tools for this play are the sounds themselves, which, through their capacity to make the imagination and inspiration of the word visible, bring to expression the *gestalt* of a thing or activity and the experience of soul associated with it.

With Eurythmy, I must go beyond the sound-gesture and create *word-gestures*. The word-gesture must transcend mere presentation of the sounds of a word, which would look like gestural spelling. It must make visible the meaning of the entire word through an artistic combination of sound gestures combined with an imagination of picture and an intuition of meaning.

The pronunciation and the meaning of the word will determine how the gesture of each individual sound will be metamorphosed, made larger or smaller, more or less stressed, shaped to interact with other sounds to make one word-picture. In their art, Eurythmists express their individual creativity through their capacity to make the imagination and the inspiration of the word reveal the true nature of the thing.

From Words to Sentences

As sounds are combined into words, words must be brought into a still higher dimension of relationship in sentences. Through an artistic use of syntax, words and phrases are ordered to create well-formed sentences.

I engage an even higher level of artistry when I create eloquent sentence-gestures that make these relationships visible. The tools I use may include specific treatments for the various parts of speech, which allow the formative forces of nouns, the activity of verbs, the relationships established by prepositions, the connectivity given by conjunctions to come alive.

The meditative imaginations written in this book provide only the first step of the journey of artistic Eurythmy. Indeed, what happens in Eurythmy when sounds are wed into words and sentences is as infinitely varied as in language.

Language is elevated into its highest dimension when it becomes poetic. The poet uses all the elements of language—sounds, words, parts of speech, rhythm, meter and stress—to create a work of art. As a Eurythmist, I take great joy in moving the elements of poetic language, but I experience prosaic or intellectual text to be unpleasant and constricting.

The Question of Different Languages

The question often arises of how to do Eurythmy in different languages. The answer is a simple one: our gestures in Eurythmy make visible precisely what we *hear*, regardless of language. What we move in Eurythmy is the actual experience of the sound itself. In principle, K is K in any language, and will be moved in the same way. Small differences may exist: a German L is different from an English L in the placement of the tongue, but even such fine differences will be made visible in movement.

More confusion may arise with the vowels, for the written signature for a vowel is often different in different languages. Whereas in English we say ā when we read the letter A, most other languages say **ah**. Nonetheless, the solution is the same: we move what we hear, and not what we read. We extend our arms wide with an open gesture when we hear the sound of wonder, **ah,** and close them firmly when we hear the sound of separation, ā.

What becomes more interesting is the question of how different languages have given different names to things. We are confronted with a living riddle when we understand that "tree" in English is "Baum" in German, "arbre" in French, "kumulaau" in Hawaiian. The English language understands trees to be tall, stretching things: the German language experiences big growths with round, generous crowns; the French speak of delicate open branches; the Hawaiian feels strong trunks and branches spread wide to the sun. We are in fact infinitely enriched when we understand the names of things in many different languages.

Biblical legend speaks of a time in the ancient past when all of humanity shared a common language. This language enabled all people to understand each other. It is said, however, that humanity of that time was too arrogant, and their aspirations too high. People began to construct a tower, the Tower of Babel, that they hoped to build all the way up to heaven. This angered Jahve and he smote the tower, and as further punishment scattered humanity to distant lands. He also took away people's capacity to understand one another, and each folk developed its own language.

I like to imagine that in those early days the words that people used were "true words," words that could completely embody the essence of meaning.

Now each separate language holds one piece of the puzzle of meaning. Through the various combinations of sounds that each language uses to describe the same object, we experience what *part* of that object that particular folk understands. When we gather all the separate words together as if we were gathering flowers for a great bouquet, the full meaning of an object shines by virtue of the beauty of all the words coming together.

Eurythmy in the World

Eurythmy on the Stage: Artistic Performances

As a performing art, Eurythmy occupies a new niche in the artistic genre. It is always performed to live poetry or to live music, and is known as Visible Speech and Visible Music.

In the case of Visible Speech, a speaker stands to the side of the stage and recites a poem or a story. A single Eurythmist or an ensemble makes visible that which is audible to the ear, through choreographed forms and expressive gestures carried out not only with the arms, but with the whole body. It is of vital importance that the speaker understands how to recite artistically, allowing the beauty of each sound, word, phrase and sentence to come alive through correct use of breathing and articulation. This will then give power and light to the feet and arms of the Eurythmist.

In the case of Visible Music, in which Eurythmy in performed to music instead of speech, one or more musicians play while the Eurythmist(s) make it "visible" on the stage. All have learned and practiced the music together, and all are able to express together—through the instrument or through gesture—the tones, intervals, dynamics and inherent "meaning" of the music.

The speakers (or musicians) and the Eurythmists experience themselves to be united in a common stream of intention, both bringing the living quality of the Word and Music to expression through their simultaneous and complementary arts. In this mystical wedding, the creativity of the speaker or musician and the Eurythmist create a new, eloquent stage art.

Eurythmy as a Healing Force: Therapeutic Eurythmy

Our bodies are temples for our spirits. For as long as we live on the earth, we use our bodies to express and unfold our destinies. The life of our soul blossoms through all the years of our life and the experiences we have through the interplay of spirit and body.

The temple of the body has been born of the same creative Word-forces that have made the world. When we are healthy, these forces exist in perfect harmony and serve us so we can experience the body as a vehicle and not as a hindrance. When we are ill, however, we are unable to use our body freely, because our constitution is manifesting some obstacle that prevents the healthy interrelationships from prevailing.

The causes of illness can occur on different levels: in the soul, as in emotional or biographical distress; in the life forces, as in a lack of vitality or hypersensitivity; or in the physical body, as in the case of an injury. In every case it is most helpful to determine at what level the illness has been caused in order to apply the best kind of treatment.

Because Eurythmy works from the core of one's being through the consciousness, soul, life, and physical bodies, it accesses sources for health that can help alleviate symptoms or even address the underlying causes for many kinds of ailments. A therapeutic Eurythmist will have studied for at least seven years to understand how to metamorphose the Eurythmy gestures of the sounds of language into the specialized therapeutic movements that have specific effects on a person's constitution. Therapeutic Eurythmy clients will be taught one sound or a series of sounds to work with intensely over an extended period of time as a personal practice, to gradually change the way they engage in their own life processes and how they feel in their body.

A healthy person will be able to freely access all the spiritual formative forces that have formed his or her body. Therapeutic Eurythmy can open the doors to this health. Physicians trained in *anthroposophical medicine* have a special insight into this field and can direct clients to practitioners.

Eurythmy and Education: Pedagogical Eurythmy

I see every young child as a fresh new visitor from the spiritual worlds. When I look into the eyes of an infant, I can see the stars shining as if I am looking into the deep canopy of the night skies.

Each child must gradually become accustomed to living on the earth. Children must gradually learn the skills of using the body, developing a sense for space, movement and balance, and large and small motor skills. They must learn to integrate the multitude of sensory experiences that come to them at every moment, and they must be able to do so effortlessly. Upon the basis of a healthy constitution they can then develop the capacities of healthy thinking, feeling and willing.

It is a wonderful thing to accompany this process with "children's," or "pedagogical" Eurythmy, an age-appropriate curriculum of Eurythmy exercises that supports and stimulates the development of the growing human being from age three through puberty and adolescence to adulthood. These Eurythmy lessons are geared to give the growing children movements that integrate body, soul and spirit in a way that will allow them to feel comfortable, coordinated, harmonious and expressive in their bodies.

These lessons are generally not long, but are rich with imagery, music, poetry and story. They have been prepared with great care so that they offer a rich variety of content and opportunity. The teacher does not explain Eurythmy, nor even offer cosmic imaginations for the sounds and experiences, but rather invites the participants to enter into the movement experience through imitation and gradual mastery of movement.

For this reason, Eurythmy has been an essential element of every Waldorf school experience for nearly 100 years, offering the somatic (body-based) component of education. Eurythmy classes not only support the development of each individual child; they also provide the opportunity for the children to grasp their academic subjects—including math, geometry, science, language arts and cultural studies—through full-body experiences.

It can only be hoped that Eurythmy will become available to more and more young people, beyond the Waldorf school curriculum.

How to use this book

This book is a collection of essays for 24 different sounds of language. Although there is an infinite number of sounds that the human voice can make, and any sound that can be spoken has a movement component that can be danced, I chose to concentrate my efforts on certain clear and archetypal sounds, regretfully leaving out many others that are also part of our everyday language.

Each essay begins with a short mantric description of the sound, followed by an imagination of the great World Creator who manifests a particular part of His/Her grandeur through the specific sound.

I then describe what I do when I prepare myself to do a sound. I become inwardly receptive in spirit, and attune myself to the being-quality of the sound, aligning myself with it. I thus engage my feeling life and let it motivate my life body, bringing me into movement. In the flow of my Eurythmy gesture I make visible the will, wisdom, movement and form of the great spirit being of the sound.

The illustrations that accompany each sound give a picture of one single moment that occurs in creating each sound. I imagine myself wearing the color of the dress. The flowing colors around the dress, the "veil," are the feeling that I experience when I immerse myself in a sound. Particular points of strength, holding and tension in my body are indicated by a third color.

It is clear that the movements of Eurythmy are not mere physical movements. They live both in the deepest core of our being, our Word-nature, and in the great world around us. When we do Eurythmy, we unite our core spirit-being with our feeling soul. We feel how our own etheric—or life—body extends into the space beyond us, and can move in a manner that overcomes the heaviness of gravity. Our Eurythmy movements are actually spirit-soul-etheric currents that we engage to fully take hold of our gestures, all the way into the finest mastery of the physical body. Through our active listening, we pour our souls into our surroundings and move what we are hearing and creatively imagining. Through our technique, we can play with gravity and levity and move the entire space around us.

When you move a sound in Eurythmy, note that you will <u>not</u> speak the sound as you move it. When you speak a sound, you pour your formative life-forces into the stream of your breath. When you do a sound-gesture in Eurythmy, you will do something radically new: you will unite your formative life-forces with the life forces around you. You will silence your throat chakra, and let will, wisdom and movement pour into your gestures.

Like many other movement disciplines popular today, such as Tai Chi, Aikido, Chi Gong, and Hula, Eurythmy is an art of the *etheric body*. Our movements live in the etheric world, and find their perfection in articulate expression in the physical world.

In contrast to most of the other disicplines, however, Eurythmy is more powerful when done indoors. In our practice, we pour our etheric body and our astral body out from ourselves and into the space we are working in, literally making the entire room we are in become the room of our soul. The walls fall away, and we feel that we are touching the stars. When we move, we play with the lines and curves of space in the room. If we work outside, however, the space feels to be too large, and we experience the lack of boundaries as if we had no skin. We disappear into the space of nature, almost as clouds disappear into the sky.

As you practice these sounds, you may begin to deepen your experience of the sounds of language. As you go through the course of your life, you may immerse yourself in the quality of the sounds, speaking them to yourself, listening to them, hearing them sparkle and crackle in other people's speech. You may look for them as formative forces in nature, finding "B" in blossoms and "K" in canyons or crystals. You can listen to the words and names of things with new interest, and discover what elements are present in your own name.

Every step of investigation can bring you nearer to new appreciations of the power and the archetype of the sound. Each sound presents you with an opportunity to grow towards something more essential, more personal, more universal.

A fully trained Eurythmist will be able to engage all aspects of his/her being in manifesting a sound. For this reason, a Eurythmy practice requires years of disciplined work, as intense as the training of a black belt in the martial arts or the attainment of a medical license as a physician. A Eurythmist must be able to know the true archetypal power of the spirit being of each sound and be able to manifest it through agile and capable movements.

Because Eurythmy is, above all, a living, spiritual art, it is my experience that electronic media are very inadequate for expressing its power and authenticity. Likewise, a book can never be a substitute for study with a living master.

Thus, I welcome you to use this book as a doorway and a source of inspiration for getting to know how the sounds of language are and feel and move. But if you are intrigued to learn more, you are encouraged to seek out a living teacher of the art.

In a Eurythmy class you will soon go far beyond the scope of this book. You will learn how to use your whole body in coordinated movements. You will learn to do not only single sounds, but how to combine the sounds into word- and eventually whole sentence-gestures. You will raise all of these to the level of artistry by moving to great poetry and story. And best of all, you will do these together with others, entering into the fascinating new experience of moving the creative Word in collaborative expression.[2]

---

[2]   Cynthia Hoven travels widely, and is available to offer workshops, seminars and private sessions. Her website eurythmyonline.com offers video instructions in how to create Eurythmy as a personal practice.She can be reached at info@eurythmonline.com.

Part Two

Making Language Visible

The Eurythmy Gestures for the Consonants and Vowels

In the following pages I present movement meditations to describe the qualities of the sounds of language. I offer a cosmic picture for each sound, and then explain how the sound thinks, feels, and is willed in us.

The soul of a Eurythmist becomes highly attuned to the relationship of sound, feeling, dynamic, color and gesture. It becomes second nature for us to feel the shapes that spoken sounds make in the air, and how the life-space of our auras moves in response. We have learned to dance with the sounds as they dance in the air. These essays are my attempt to open to you a doorway into a deeper understanding and experience of the sounds that have made the world and live on in your body and your soul.

The Sequence of the Gestures: Cosmic Correspondences

Twelve particular constellations, known as the *zodiac,* encircle the earth as a starry belt. These twelve define the ecliptic, or the path of the earth and the planets in relationship to the sun. For that reason, these constellations have a particular formative presence in our universe. Their relative movements can be experienced as an ever-changing dance or conversation.

Legends from the dawn of time describe spiritual beings who walked through the skies. Great gods and goddesses, including Cassioepeia, Orion, Hercules and others can be found in the various star formations. In long distant ages, we could experience fellowship with the beings of the starry world, and addressed them as gods and goddesses. In this sense, the constellations of the zodiac were experienced to be populated by animals and gods, archetypal figures who ruled our life on earth.

Out of his spiritual research, Rudolf Steiner also recognized the living quality of the zodiac circle. He experienced it speaking or singing to us, and perceived that a specific consonant or consonant pair sounds out of each sign of the zodiac. These signify the cosmic formative forces that surround our earth.

I have selected seventeen consonants to describe in these essays, and arranged them in the order of their zodiacal sequence, traveling through the cycle from Aries to Pisces.

Aries (The Ram)	W,V
Taurus (The Bull)	R
Gemini (The Twins)	H
Cancer (The Crab)	F
Leo (The Lion)	D,T
Virgo (The Virgin)	B,P
Libra (The Scales)	C (ts)
Scorpio (The Scorpion)	S
Sagittarius (The Archer)	G,K
Capricorn (The Sea-Goat)	L
Aquarius (The Waterman)	M
Pisces (The Fish)	N

Likewise, each of the planets sings to the earth with a different vowel quality. I have chosen seven vowels to describe, corresponding to the sun, the moon and five planets.

Sun	Au
Moon	EI (i)
Venus	A (ah)
Mars	E (ā)
Mercury	I (ē)
Jupiter	O (oh)
Saturn	U(oo)

The Gestures of the Consonants

W

Pronounced "wuh"

THE WORLD WORD WEAVES THROUGH THE WORLD.

The first utterance of the World Word arose as an expression of pure world will and wisdom. It rose as the surge of a wave from the depths of the spirit's ocean being, and in its wake the world was born.

W is the wave that rises from the depths of the water, and the wind that blows through the widths of the world.

Intention

In the Being of **W**, I discover the guardian of the World Word. It is the delicate breath that hovers at the threshold between spirit and matter.

Feeling

I stand clothed in deep blue, experiencing the peace of the world. Around me I sense the pale yellow field of world movement, pregnant with surging life.

Movement and Form

I bend myself low to the ground and let my arms hang heavy at my sides with the palms facing behind me, containing a quiet violet tension in the backs of my arms.
Feeling the impulse of a wave swelling from the depth below me I rise,
lifting my arms with a movement that starts from the shoulders. My arms press outwards and forwards in a great convex curve. The movement expands and grows around me.

Soul Response

I have become upright. My head, no longer bent to the earth, is crowned with yellow light. All around me I feel spirit brightness. I experience the wonder of being human.

Small wonders: Winter warblers watch for wiggly worms.

V

I AM ENVELOPED BY VEILS OF LIVING LOVE.

The Will of the Creator reverberates through the universe, a vast wave of spirit warmth and love.

*V is the partner sound of **W**. **W** is the undersurface of a wave and **V** its undulation as it ripples across the surface. Through **V**, the World Word makes manifest the world.*

Intention

In the Being of V, I ride along the rolling surface of the World Word, surfing the cresting wave as it unfolds the stream of world becoming.

Feeling

In deep blue I rest in the peace of the world, sensing myself surrounded by a gentle lilac ocean. I stand in silence, waiting. Behind me a great wave begins to rise and move towards me. I lift my arms lightly onto the surface of the water, feeling the movement ready to break over my head.

Movement and Form

Lifting my arms behind me, I dive into the waves of world becoming. Leading with my fingertips, I follow the movement of the cresting wave over the top of my head and onwards into the space before me, rising and falling in voluptuous ripples. I feel myself to be just below the surface of the running wave. The wave moves on, far beyond me, into distant space. I hold red tension in my legs, my sternum, my shoulders, and the top of my head, but my arms are fluid and their movement flows smoothly.

Soul Response

As the wave of movement moves above me and through me, I am enveloped by the wisdom of the world. The dome of my head mirrors the vault of the heavens: I am crowned by the lilac wave.

Small wonders: Quivering violin voices reverberate around very velvety violets.

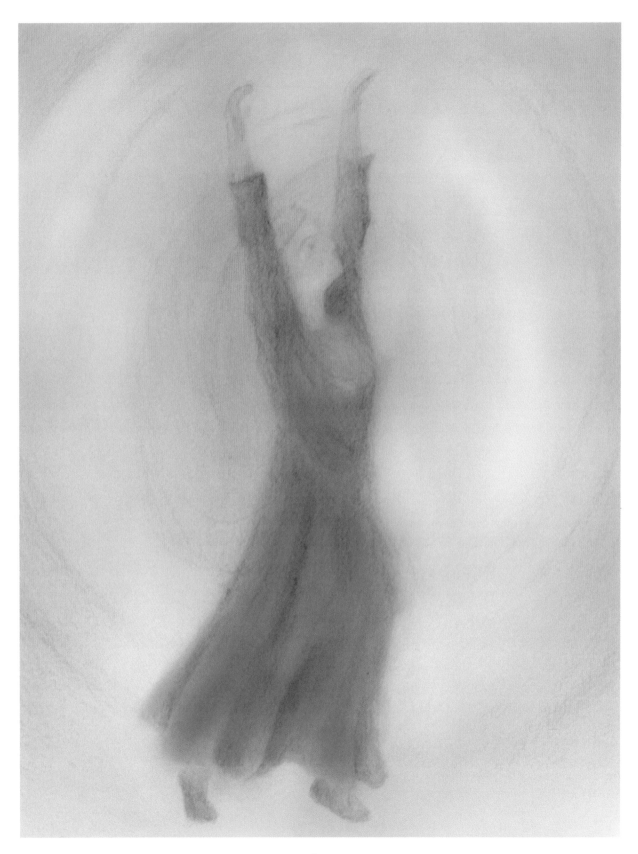

R

FORCES OF RENEWAL LEAD ME TO REJUVENATION AND REBIRTH.

The breath of the Creator lives in the element of air as it permeates the world and creates dynamic and changing relationships. Its movement turns things inside out and upside down, causing reversals and inversions. Nothing can withstand its dynamic force; neither that which is fiery or fluid, nor even that which is hardened and brittle.

R is an irresistible yellow wind that surrounds the glowing red of fire. Through R we are released from the old and prepared for the new. R lifts us out of sedentary states and sweeps us along, as the wind tosses tumbleweed or whips through the trees. Through its power, we may be coaxed into running or thrown into cartwheels and somersaults. Breathing deeply, we are filled with the vibrant joy of movement.

Intention

In the Being of R, I will find the power that lifts me beyond all inertia. I open myself to the power of all-engaging change.

Feeling

I am robed in red, charged with power and intensity. Around me surges radiant movement, yellow, weightless and free. I invite this yellow to take hold of my soul and my body. I will bring this Irresistible movement into every least part of my self. The tension in my arms is green, offering form but no resistance to the movement that will play with me.

Movement and Form

I lift my arms lightly before me, bent at the elbow and parallel, and prepare my legs to engage in movement by stepping forward with one foot. As I engage the power of R, I allow my arms to circle around, sinking downwards towards the floor, rising behind me to the zenith above my head, and sinking once again. The revolving movement can go on and on forever. It can also reverse directions or go from side to side. As it engages my legs, I take light-filled steps. The activity of R is self-perpetuating.

Soul response

As my soul experiences the release into vigorous movement, it finds joy. Into the very cells of my body, I feel the lightness of air. My eyes sparkle, my soul wants to laugh. I feel life.

Small wonders: Rushing rivers refresh, rivulets ripple and run.

H

Pronounced "ha"

I EXHALE AND INHALE THE BREATH OF THE SPIRIT.

With the first divine exhalation, the world burst open, and all that would ever become poured forth. Creation began. At the end of time, the Creator will inhale and call the world back into its heart.

H is the breath of spirit, the hallowed sound of the holy World-Word. H becomes manifest at the subtle threshold between spirit and matter.

Intention

In the Being of **H**, I find the delicate presence of the spirit, exhaling and inhaling, opening and closing.

Feeling

(Out-breathing **H**): Yellow with light, I gather my forces and feel myself pregnant with being,.
My arms are quietly crossed, with blue muscle tension.
(In-breathing **H**): In radiant yellow, I feel myself expanded in the space around me,
and prepare myself to draw the breath of spirit into myself.

Movement and Form

I begin with my arms crossed, perhaps with my hands balled into fists with blue muscle tension . Engaging my shoulder blades, I open my arms wide to the right and the left. My gesture begins with force, filling he space around me with soft red vigor. As my arms continue to open, my feeling extends and reaches into the far distances of space. Blue tension allows me to stay in myself and not completely dissolve.

Alternately, I begin with my arms opened wide above me, and then decisively but lightly contract them, pulling them towards me and perhaps even crossing them and creating fists. The dynamic then becomes soft as it comes to rest in quiet blue.

Soul response

I feel my soul fully open and joyous. I am freed to soar.
Alternately, I come to rest within myself, feeling myself newly invigorated with the fresh energy
I have taken hold of and received into myself.

Small wonders: Holy happiness heals me and makes me whole.

F

I FREE THE FORCE OF KNOWLEDGE INTO FLOW OF AIR.

The fire of spirit flames forth through all of existence. The Creator reveals itself in a primal outpouring of pure will, and out of this fire-force the world springs into existence. In every act of spirit creating, this primal fire-force is present, vessel for the love and wisdom of the Creator.

In its flight, F bears wisdom in its heart and on its wings. The Creator has laid the fire of spirit into the human race. Bearing original will and wisdom, we have received the ability to send forth this spirit fire-force through our spoken word, our exhaled breath, our out-flowing will. We become aware that it is the Creator's own wisdom that permeates our breathing, speaking and actions.

Intention

In the Being of **F**, I experience the fiery force of creative will filling me and flowing forth from me.

Feeling

As a vessel for the spirit, I have received world wisdom into myself. Selflessly white in pure consciousness of what I know, but empowered with red muscle tension, I will free the force of knowledge into the flow of air with bright orange flames.

Movement and Form

I draw my arms back behind me, bent at the elbow, and feel myself taut as a bowstring. I open my awareness to the space behind me. As I release the tension, an imaginary arrow flies forth from my bow. Sometimes I shoot forward with one strong **F**, and sometimes I can experience a series of short bursts with several small **F**'s that dance through the air as stones skip across water.

Soul response

Through my movements, the ripened forces of my own soul life fill the air around me. I experience them as they expand into the periphery, until at length they dissipate and dissolve in the distance.

Small wonders: Finely freckled fairies flit about with fantastic feathers; fierce falcons fly far.

D

DOWNWARD DRAWN, I DESCEND INTO THE DEPTHS.

The World Creator separated the heavens from the earth with the power of D. The earth and the water elements were compressed downward, into realms of darkness. Above them, the starry world shone brightly, freed from the dross of matter.

*The dark **D** defines the realms of earth.*

Intention
In the Being of **D**, I experience the power of the World Creator Spirit who defines the dimensions of space, creating the polarity of space above and space below.

Feeling
Radiant with orange, I gather my intention to separate weight from levity, darkness from light. I am aware of the tension of duality and polarity. I will actively separate the realms of heaven and earth, pushing downwards from the heights into the depths.

Movement and Form
I lift my arms to my shoulder height and rest them in the air. With the fire of red-orange power all around me but soft lilac pressure in my muscles, I push downwards through space, compacting the field below me. I experience the counter movement of forces rising through my upright posture, and I stand taller. With the palms of my hand flat and grounded feet firmly on the earth, I stand rooted in place.

Soul response
I feel the power of being grounded through my whole being. I find strength in my lower body, and simultaneously attain light and clarity in my consciousness.

Small wonders: Dastardly dirty Danny digs deep dark dugouts.

d

DAINTY AND DELICATE DETAILS SURROUND ME.

*Free of the dark realms of the earth, with the delicate d we direct our souls
to the wonders that are all around.*

The soft d dances with delightful levity and grace.

Intention

I open my mind and see the wonders of the created world around me.

Feeling

Robed in orange, I awaken keen interest in all the things of the world. My attention
floods the space with soft vermillion intensity.

Movement and Form

I lift my arms and awaken my experience in my fingertips with soft reddish-lilac sensitivity.
I point my hands with delicate gestures , in any direction, indicating the blossoms,
beasts, and stars that I can feel around me.

Soul Response

I have joyfully immersed myself in the sense world. The handiwork of the Creator
that surrounds me on all sides awakens my delight in the world.

Small wonders: Dazzling daffodils drizzle dewdrops.

T

TOUCHED BY THE SPIRIT, I AM TRANSFORMED BY TRUTH.

In constant world creating, the Creator summons all of its Universal Power and hurls bolts of red-hot lightning into the earth, striking to the core of every manifest thing. The power of the Spirit re-enlivens the lifeless world of matter.

T is the masculine counterpart of *D*. It gathers and directs both the force of spirit power and the light of spirit consciousness. In the human being, *T* is the pre-cursor to manifestation of the individual self-conscious *I* (ee), or I-Am. In ancient times, a person touched by the might of spirit would be thrown to the ground or knocked unconscious. The modern human being can invoke the *T* and be strengthened by it.

Intention

In the Being of **T**, I will unite myself with the lightning power of the Creator that directs the entire force of the Creative Will into the core of my being.

Feeling

I seek to unite myself with the powers of the universe. Clothed in orange, I stand surrounded by light and feel the red power of spirit all around me. I open the deepest parts of my soul and offer myself to the highest I can imagine. The tension in my arms is green, offering form but no resistance to the powerful forces around me.

Movement and Form

I lower my arms to my sides, and let my intention reach into my fingertips. I radiantly lift my arms as wide and as high as I can. Where they meet above my head, I invite world-spirit-light to strike into me. With the backs of my hands together, my fingertips forcefully strike the top of my head at the point of the crown chakra. I stand upright at the moment of impact, strengthened in posture from head to foot.

Soul Response

Were the bones of my skull not so hard and were I not so dull in spirit, I would be thrown to the ground with the force of the impact of the **T**. My hardness, however, protects me, so I can withstand the power of the lightning force streaming into my body. As it enters through the head and reverberates through the sacred centers of my body, it resounds at my throat, my heart, my solar plexus, the base of my spine, my knees. I am ablaze with spirit fire and filled with green vital force.

Small wonders: Tall trees' tender twigs try to tickle tiny tots.

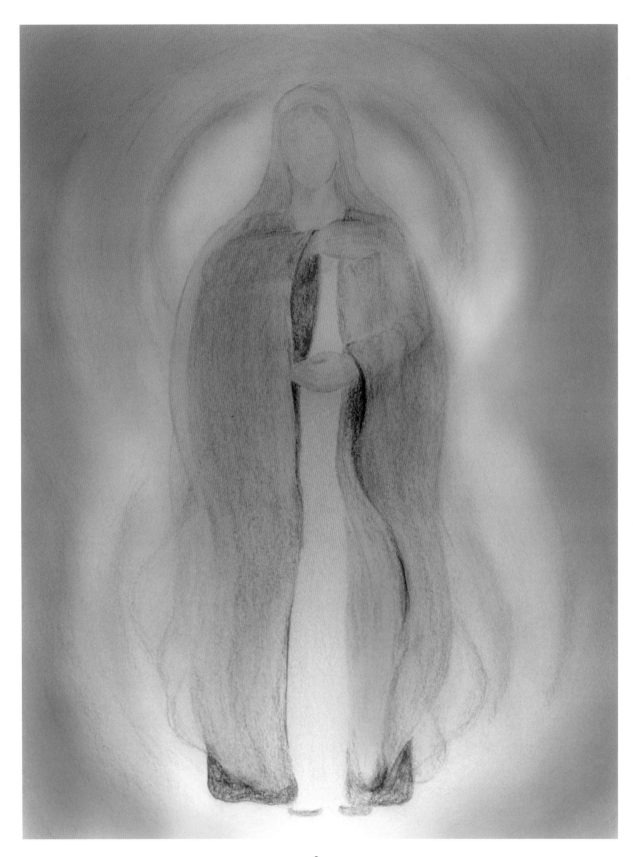

B
I FEEL SAFE BOUNDARIES IN THE WARM EMBRACE OF THE SPIRIT.

Feeling love, the creator wraps its limitless Being around the entirety of all that is, all that has been and all that will ever be in a cloak of soft sky blue. We are forever held, in a mantle of endless maternal love.

B is the gesture of the arms of embrace that wrap themselves around all things. As your angel holds you warm, as a mother cradles a child, so we are held in the embrace of the great cosmic spirit. I can explore big and bold B's, and also little-bitty B's. I can make B before me, behind me, above me, below me: I can discover B with my hands and with my legs. In nature I can find the gesture of the B in all the round things of the world: boulders, bees and blossoms. B protects the small tender things of the world, wrapping itself around babies and embryos.

Intention
In the Being of B, I discover the intention of the World Creator to pour forth all that it harbors within and give birth to it. The World Creator will hold the universe in loving embrace, now and for all time.

Feeling
I joyously and trustingly open my soul, radiating yellow light. I reach out my arms and invoke a cloak of warmth and protection that will descend and wrap itself around me. The spiritual world fills my outstretched arms with a rich blue cloak, present as it has always been since the beginning of time to hold the world. My cloak has a red lining which will give me firm boundaries and strength. The B will create a safe wall around me, a place of protection that will give me form and definition.

Movement and Form
I stand grounded on the earth, and expand my arms. When my feeling reaches my fingertips, they touch two great blue curving surfaces, right and left. I pull them in from both sides, wrapping myself in a cloak of protection. The strong red in my arms pushes against the blue, preventing it from pressing too tightly around me.

Soul response
I am the angel that protects my self. I am the mother that holds the child, and I am the child that is held by the mother. My soul rests in the knowledge that it is safe when it makes boundaries. The B has taught me how the Creator has made the universe and holds it in love.

Small wonders: Behold beauty in birds, bubbles, blossoms and bumblebees.

49

P

IN THE PRESENCE OF SPIRIT, I PRAY FOR PEACE.

The Spirit protects all the creatures of the world. Heavenly forces press in upon the earth from all sides, holding, sculpting and shaping it.

P is the masculine counterpart of B, a stronger, more robust force. In B I invite the embrace of the Mother to hold me: in P I actively draw the form-giving power of the world towards me, and feel its support as it presses and compresses me, defining me from without. I respond to the pressure of the P with a gesture that springs outward again.

P is found in things that pop open. Whereas bubbles burst, seedpods must pop.

Intention

In the Being of P, I know the power of the World Creator to forcefully press in upon me, forming and holding me. I welcome the gentle sculpting forces that will give me definition and protection.

Feeling

Clothed in soft blue, I open myself and invoke a gentle lilac-red glow around me. I reach out my arms towards the heavens and from the stars I receive in my right and left hands luminous rose red veils.

Movement and Form

Standing tall, I lift my right and left arms to the sides. As I lift them, the lilac of the space around me gives way to red. My fingertips touch the inner surface of a sphere that surrounds me on all sides, and I draw it towards me by pulling my arms back in to my sides with soft blue-green muscle tension: they bend at the elbows and wrists. When the contraction reaches its culmination, I release the tension in my shoulders, elbows and wrists, as well as in my legs, and the lilac-red veil floats outward again.

Soul Response

I have clothed myself in the spirit, and rest in its peace and strength.

Small wonders: The princess prepares herself with perfume and purple peacock feathers to meet the perfect prince.

C

(pronounced "ts")

I DANCE WITH CELESTIAL GRACE.

In the fire and the smoke of incense, the sacrificial offerings ascend to heaven. Everything that has taken on form and fallen into gravity can be transformed through fire back to spirit.

*There exists a force of levity that overcomes the burden of gravity. **C** enters into the roots of things and lifts them lightly into the air. It dances through the world, delighting in the forces of resurrection and life.*

Although little used in English, C is a sound of joy and surprise, offering to us the happiness of overcoming the heaviness of the earth.

Intention
In the Being of C, I unite myself with the process of transformation, ascending from the depths of weight into the heights.

Feeling
In quiet blue, I bend myself to the earth. Suddenly I feel my heaviness give way to light, and I become robed in the lightness of yellow. The air around me sparkles with orange. I will lift my arms into the air, delighting in the forces of weightlessness. There is a gentle lilac tension in my arms.

Movement and Form
I spread my arms wide and then sink into my knees, bringing my arms to my sides. Keeping my palms facing upwards, I bring my hands together, as if I were gathering an armful of flowers, and then lightly toss my hands upwards, as if the flowers were flying up into the air. Again and again, I gather and toss, rising and straightening as I go. I end fully upright with my arms high in the air.

Soul Response
In the work of transforming matter I have transformed my own self.

Small Wonders: Dancers celebrate with sizzling excitement.

S

I SUBDUE THE SNAKE AND I MASTER THE STAFF.

The serpent slipped into the garden of Eden and enticed the first couple to take the fruit of the tree of knowledge. Tasting the sense world, they found themselves stripped of their innocence and cast forth from paradise, facing a future of struggle and suffering.

Formerly upright, the snake that once seduced us now slithers on the ground, the lowliest of creatures, until one day it will be raised again through our activity and transformed into a noble staff of knowledge. A mercurial shape-shifter, S can assume any form and dance with any movement. The gesture for S will be discovered every time anew, as it twists and turns with sinuous curves. The magician and the healer must hold inner stillness in themselves to allow the S to unfold around them. The S is the power of the Kundalini, the fire-force that rises snake-like along the spine. It is the Staff of Caduceus, the two-headed snake wrapped around a staff.

Intention

In the Being of S, I confront the power of world intelligence that has been woven into all the things of the world. I prepare myself for the confrontation with the sacred forces of death, healing, and resurrection.

Feeling

Clothed in the gray robes of the shape-shifter, I stand in a field of brown, the color of spun-gold. Standing tall, I invoke the highest power of my ego, and prepare to wield my strength as I engage with the sinuous mercurial forces of the snake. My spine is my reference point in the middle of the swirling movement. With the force of S, I will be able to trace any and all shapes in the universe. Through learning to dance with the snake, I will gain understanding.

Movement and Form

With neutral black tension, I stretch out my arms. I have the greatest imaginable freedom with the S to describe any shape in space, linear or curved, ascending or descending. If the snake that I hold is tame, my S may be a lemniscate that circles around me. If it is wild, my gesture will curve and bend in dynamic asymmetry.

Soul Response

I have summoned great powers and wielded them with might. As the movement subsides, I feel the afterglow of inner strength, calm and consolidated. Strong silence surrounds me.

Small wonders: Silvery slivers stream and sparkle.

G

As in "golden"

THROUGH THE GRACE OF GOD I GROW TOWARDS GOODNESS.

*With the power of **G**, the Creator opens wide the gates of the universe. Golden glowing light pours outwards, creating and illuminating the entire universe.*

***G** is the sound that enables us to open the doors of our souls, that we may overcome our limitations and perceive new vistas and possibilities.*

Intention

In the Being of **G**, I push open the gates that separate me from clear vision of my future growth and goals.

Feeling

I experience my soul as if surrounded by a cocoon. Delicate silver-gray mists are wrapped around me, and the light of my spirit glows with soft yellow light. I feel the longing to free myself from my cocoon and move towards an as yet unknowable future. I am ready to move from inward quiet towards outward expression.

Movement and Form

Standing straight, I draw my arms together, crossing one over the other with elbows bent and the inner surfaces of the upper and lower arms and hands facing outward. Inhaling, I focus gentle blue tension in the large muscles of my upper arms, and push outwards to the right and left.

The muscle tension is echoed in the legs as well. A bright space opens up between my arms, and my heart feels freedom in the space before me. I keep my arms held apart, as if I am holding a door open.

Soul response

The possibilities of my future are now visible to the open gaze of my heart and eye. I can envision my life's goals, my wishes and dreams, and I trust that there is a road for me to walk. My soul forces have been consolidated, and I am strengthened in my inner capacity to identify and engage my force of will to push aside obstacles.

Small wonders: Golden-eyed grasshoppers jump through the grass, giving us great glee.

K

I BEHOLD THE CRYSTAL CLEAR CONTOURS OF THE CREATED WORLD.

*With the power of **K**, the World Creator compresses the fiery spirit into sharp contours and crystalline forms. Primal fire, light and movement come to an abrupt halt: the solid earth element is born.*

*K is the masculine counterpart of **G**. It makes manifest a decisive gesture of will, a sharp and certain cleavage, a power that brooks no compromise. It defines the bedrock of all being.*

Intention
In the Being of **K**, I experience forces that cut, cleave, compress, consolidate. I can invoke this power to create my mark in the world with crystal clarity.

Feeling
I choose to break free of limitations and dissolve my barriers. I invoke the red-hot power of the warrior in me. I have the strength to express my inner intentions outwardly. My movements are like flashing yellow swords.

Movement and Form
I lift my arms into the air, poised with red power and anticipation. I envision my walls, my blockages, and the new forms I will create, and concentrate my power into my upper arms. I exert a sharp, clear, downward or outward impact on the space around me. My entire body holds itself taut in a self-determined form. My arms reverberate with the power they have exerted: my muscle tension is vermillion.

Soul response
I am strong, clear and confident. I am capable of clarity and of making a mark on the world.

Small wonders: Courteous courtesans carry the king's kites with courage!

L

TRANSFORMATION LEADS ME INTO LIGHT, LOVE AND LIFE.

Having fallen out of luminous spirit heights, forces of death and darkness have descended into the realm of earth. Feeling love and affirming light, the World Creator reaches into the depths to lead it back to spirit union. The waters of life move through eternal cycles of resurrection and transformation.

L is found in everything that moves through death and life. Its gesture guides the changing of the seasons, the cycles of evaporation and precipitation, the flow of fluids passing through plant life, and the cycles of dying and becoming. No death is too dark, no destruction so great that the forces of Spirit cannot reach into them and transform them. L changes darkness into light, destruction into love, death into life.

Intention
In the Being of **L**, I engage the force of life that will bring rejuvenation to all that is stagnant within and around me.

Feeling
In the world of matter, I am poised between polarities. The endless cycle of life and death, matter and spirit, metamorphosis and transformation accompany my life. In the **L**, I participate in the cycling of creation. I stand clothed in silver-gray, surrounded by the gentle lilac-colored field of life.

Movement and Form
With golden-orange lightness in my joints and muscles, I lift my arms to the sides with my palms down, sensing an imaginary horizon line between gravity below and light above. With rounded arms, I reach into the depths, bring my hands together, and lift them side by side before me. They pass the horizon lines and rise further, into realms of light and weightlessness, as plants are lifted to the sun. At the zenith, my gesture opens as a blossoming flower. I keep my palms facing upwards as I open my arms wide and let them sink lightly to the horizon. Creating a new L, I turn my palms downwards once again and I reach into the depths, entering a new cycle of metamorphosis.

Soul response
In the repeating cycles, I find the strength to meet depression and despair, to engage in the descent into matter, and to actively participate in the never ending cycles of change, growth and metamorphosis.
I change, and I am changed.

Small wonders: Lovely little lizards leap and laugh around lily pads.

M

I MOVE WITHIN MIGHTY CURRENTS OF WARMTH THAT MOLD THE WORLD.

The heart of the Creator permeates the entire living universe with its divine essence in constant self-awareness and self-creating. The living universe breathes, and its breathing can be perceived everywhere one looks, listens and feels. In M the moving breath of the Creator manifests as ever-present streams of warmth, and all of living Creation silently resounds with an eternal aummmm.

M is both peaceful and intense. Just as M needs the intensity of lips pressed firmly together to be articulated, in Eurythmy it can only be moved with steady pressure at the surface of the skin. M creates and nurtures through warmth and intimacy.

Intention

In the Being of M, I find the eternal presence of the Creator Spirit who enlivens, en-souls, and penetrates the universe with warmth and love.

Feeling

I am robed in peaceful green as I open myself to the etheric world of life. I open myself to perceive the space around me filled with liquid blue currents of flowing life. I hold a violet colored tension in my arms, my shins, the small of my back and my forehead, denoting quiet and intensity.

Movement and Form

Parallel M: I lift my arms, bending them at the elbow and holding the lower arms close to my upper body, palms forward. In lifting, I inhale and invite a flood of warmth to flow through me from behind. I am caught up in the forward-moving current and enter into the exhaling movement. At first my lower arms and then my hands lead the movement, as if I am breathing out through them as I feel my way into space. At length, when my arms are fully extended, my palms and then my fingertips lay themselves flat into space. Both my forehead and my lower legs gently echo this forward movement. I increase my tension in the small of my back by rounding slightly backwards. I can then turn my hands around and let them come back towards my chest. Alternately, I can sensitively descend into the depths or rise upwards into the heights with a falling or rising M.

Opposite M: I lift both hands to my chest level, with one close to my body as above, and the other extended before me. The palms of the hands face each other. Two streams of warmth approach me, from before and from behind. I move my hands towards, past and beyond each other. Each arm reaches the end of its extension as the movement breathes out and through me. I turn my hands around again so they face toward each other once more. Again and again my arms can move through the space, tasting and savoring it with lively sensing of warmth and being.

Soul response

Concentrating my forces, I learn to perceive and become one with the breathing of the world-aummm.

I am surrounded by warmth. I am calm.

Small wonders: In the midst of miracles and mystery, we may find minor magic in mice, mists and mischief.

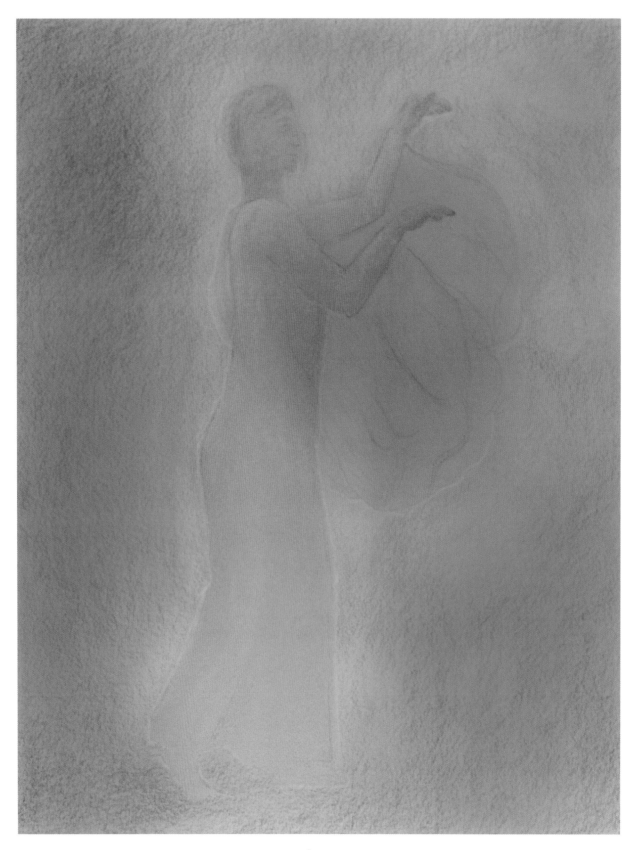

N

I HAVE NEED OF SEPARATION TO GAIN KNOWLEDGE.

The Creator shaped the manifest world with sensitive hands and then drew back, revealing the myriad shapes of the manifest world. The Creator granted independence to the physical world, allowing it to be separate, in order that knowledge and freedom might arise.

N is the gesture of touching the world to perceive it, and then retreating into oneself to reflect and gain knowledge. N is also negativity and annihilation.

Intention

In the Being of N, I will awaken, to feel my separation from the divine.

Feeling

Clothing myself in yellow-green, I feel my way into the quiet yet intense blue-violet space around me. I awaken delicate sensitivity in my hands and fingers, with bright lilac muscle tension. My sensitivity to the space around me is heightened.

Movement and Form

I gently lift my arms and reach them forwards, allowing an infinitely tender tension to awaken in my hands and fingers. Reaching an imagined object, I abruptly pull back, as if my fingertips had touched a hot stove. I quickly regain my composure, and stand as if suspended in space for a moment, holding the form, the shape, the memory of what I had met. For a moment my movement is arrested in the air, and I feel light tension in my fingertips and the back of my head.

Soul Response

I awaken through a stronger sense of self and world, and my perception of things in the sense world is strengthened. I know the importance of the power of separation, antipathy, and negation. The sum total of all the parts of knowledge will rebuild the divine unity of the World-All in the fullness of time, with all humans united in conscious understanding.

Small Wonders: No! Never! Nothing! Nada! Nein!

The Gestures of the Vowels

AU
THOU, O LORD, ART MIGHTY. AUM, AMEN.

The mighty sound AU marks the beginning and ending of all things. Through the openness of the Ah, the Creator let His exalted essence flow outwards, creating the great beings of the universe and all time, space and matter. So, too, at the end of time, all things will be called back to the heart of the Creator, through the power of the U(oo).

In the mighty gesture of AU, we raise ourselves to honor and adore the Creator of all. This can also be echoed in a small au, through which we behold the handwork of the creator in all the wonders of the world, right into the tiniest flowers and miracles of nature, right into the human heart.

Intention
In the Being of AU, I will know the sun-nature of my own heart, which harbors the light of the spirit and radiates through me into the world.

Feeling
I fill my heart with love and reverence for the Creator of all. With a heart filled with gratitude and bright with gold, I stand in the radiant white field of the infinite and open my arms, as if in a grand salutation to the rising sun.

In finding the microcosmic au, I lay my two hands on my heart in devotion, or perhaps upon my head as if wearing a crown.

Movement and Form
Moving out from my heart center, I lift one arm in the angle of the sound Ah above my head, and lift my other arm to parallel it as in an OO.

Soul Response
The AU elevates me beyond the concerns of everyday affairs and raises me in prayer and praise to the Divine.

EI (I)

I FIND MYSELF IN THE BRIGHT LIGHT OF DAY AND THE QUIET SILENCE OF THE NIGHT.

In the diphthong **I**, the firm contours of the world dissolve in misty movements, stream in fluid currents. Layers move across layers, membranes slide across membranes. Alone among the major vowels, the **I** is not fixed, but glides and slides in constantly changing forms.

In the English language, the ego rises to self-awareness through calling itself "**I**." The English experience of self loses itself by immersing itself in the world: emerging, it has attained self-awareness.

Intention

In the Being of **I**, **I** will slip into the subtle levels of fluid vitality that weave through the world.

Feeling

I am robed in violet, feeling a quiet concentration of my forces. All around me is silvery light, subtle and mysterious as moonlight upon snow. I cannot control this light: it beckons me to become alert in all my senses, to listen and feel into the space around me. I move through this magical world with a gentle sliding motion.

Movement and Form

In English, the sound **I** is made of a fluid combination of Ah and Ē. I shift my weight and lift my arms lightly to one side. They are slightly open, forming a gentle, weightless Ah. Both palms face the same direction, either up or down. I am clothed in violet, feeling a quiet intensity. Sensitive to a silver light all around me, I allow my arms to glide from one side to the other. The outer arm crosses above the lower until they pass my midline: at that point, the lower arm overtakes the first, and glides further until it rings into space with a gentle Ē.

The **I** may move from right to left, from left to right, from above below or from below above.

Soul Response

I experience a gentle fluidity and a heightened sensitivity to my environment as I move into and through the silvery space around me. The **I** inspires gentleness, so that I do not disturb the magic that surrounds me.

71

A (AH)

I OPEN MY HEART IN AWE AND WONDER.

When we speak of paradise, our imagination evokes for us a beautiful and glorious landscape. Rich and verdant forests offer succulent fruits, and the scents of fragrant flowers fill the air with odors that delight us. Animals are tame and live in harmony with one another and with human beings. We walk upon the dew-sprinkled earth with amazement and reverential gratitude. We experience paradise anew every time we stand open-hearted before the Creator and take all the beauty of the world into ourselves.

Every child is born upon the earth in a condition of paradise, with an open heart and open gaze. This is the openness of the sound Ah. It is this utterly vulnerable receptivity of the naked soul that we must find to express the sound Ah in Eurythmy.

Ah also expresses the soul that awakens to the world in the act of perceiving.

Intention

In the Being of Ah, I will open my heart completely.

Feeling

I stand in stillness, emptying my heart of impure feelings. Clothing myself in a strong, life-affirming reddish-lilac, I feel vital forces surging through me. I become aware of the stars, sun and moon above me, of the realms of life all around me, of the rich earth below me, and I desire to become a vessel to be filled by them. The beauty of the sense world surrounds me as a blue-green field of living forces. I center my feeling in my heart, and open myself to be a vessel for the spirit and the world.

Movement and Form

I extend my arms fully into an open gesture. The angle I choose is neither too large nor too small, but corresponds in feeling to the size of the angle my throat makes when I speak Ah. I straighten the muscles of my arms with a reddish tension in order that I can receive and take hold of the in-streaming forces. The base of the angle my arms make is in my spine: the center of it is my heart.

The gesture of the Ah may be made towards any height – above, in the middle, or down. The shape created becomes a chalice, filled by forces flowing to it from afar – from the stars, from the middle realm, from the earth.

Soul Response

I have unlocked the forces within me of pure innocence and receptivity. The world has created me and filled me. I am open as on the first of days, and I am strong.

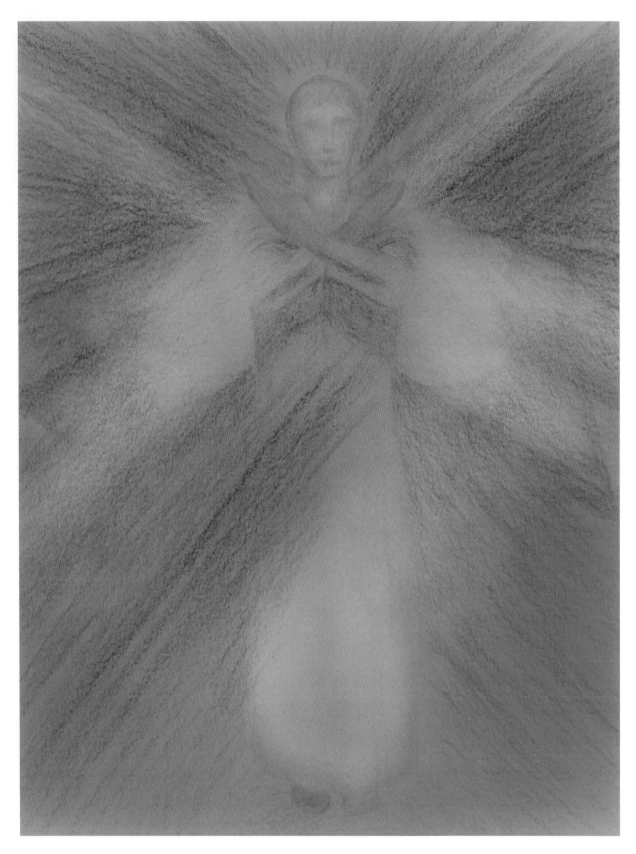

E (Ā)

I CREATE SEPARATION AND SAFETY.

Humanity did not remain in the divine paradise of innocence. We ate of the fruits of the world, and we became entangled in the world of the senses, marveling in its delights and longing to be filled by it. At length, however, our paradisiacal union with creation came to an end. Separated, we received the dual gifts of independence and pain. We discovered boundaries and focus, clarity and reason.

So, too, every child awakens from the divine oneness with the spiritual world and the earthly union with the mother, to begin his or her own individual journey. Soon the visual axis crosses, the hands grasp one another, and the world comes into focus. The process of distinguishing self from the surroundings begins. This is the rightful strength of the sound Ā.

Intention

In the Being of Ā, I will find strength through creating boundaries.

Feeling

After experiencing the openness of the Ah, I long to come more to myself by establishing a threshold in front of me, or a wall around me. I peacefully stand clothed in quiet green, and draw bright rays of yellow light to me. I press one arm against the other where they cross, and reinforce it with red firmness. I close the gates and experience the membrane of self and world.

Movement and Form

I lift my arms into openness, and find the two streams of movement coming towards me. If these are in the zone of my heart, they will cross before my chest; if they are above me, they will cross above my head; if they are below me they will cross before my legs. In some instances, I may even cross my legs in Ā. Wherever the crossing is, I reinforce it with a light red muscle tension, pressing one limb into the other.

Soul Response

I feel the power of having rightful boundaries that protect me from being overwhelmed by outside influences. I have strength, focus, and well-being.

I (Ē)

I FEEL MYSELF IN BALANCE BETWEEN HEAVEN AND EARTH.

When we humans first left paradise, we defined ourselves by what we were not, experiencing the separation of the Ā. In time, however, we awakened to our own spiritual nature, and through spiritual self-knowledge knew ourselves to be bearers of the World Word. This spirit self is the Ego, the I-Am, and its invisible fuel is the essence of spirit-being. .

So, too, in the course of each human life, we can evolve past the immature experience of defining ourselves by what we are not, and begin to define ourselves from within. The Ego, the I-Am of the human being is the eternal flame that burns in the inner core of our being. It is never in a stagnant condition. In constant self-creating, it lives in the dynamic relationship between being and non-being, interior and exterior, right and left, up and down, heaven and earth. As if on a tightrope, the I-Am seeks and creates balance between polarities. I create myself anew whenever I awaken into self-consciousness. The sound Ē rings forth from my soul when it manifests its own light-being in spirit filled self-manifestation.

Intention
In the Being of Ē, I will radiantly shine from out of the core of my being.

Feeling
Clothed in radiant yellow-orange, I feel my heart, the center of my being. A stream of light radiates outward from this center with energetic red brilliance, expanding outwards through one arm into the space around me. I balance this outgoing energy with a blue counterweight in my other arm. I feel the dynamic tension of the forces of heaven and earth (or any other polarities) working through me, and I create the balance between the two.

Movement and Form
I begin by feeling the flame in my heart, the center of my being, and prepare to send it into my arms. The movement and dynamic of the two arms balance each other in speed and power. The arm that experiences the heavy counterweight may be lightly clenched in a fist.

Soul Response
In creating the balance between polarities, I find the light and joy of spirit activity in myself.

O (OH)

I HOLD THE BELOVED WORLD IN THE EMBRACE OF MY ARMS.

We as humanity now stand at the point when each one of us, as an individual human being, must overcome our separateness and evolve to the stage where we can understand and love all of humanity and the earth. Self-realized human beings now experience the need to step into a new and loving relationship with the world from which we are born.

The strivings of a mature human being no longer seek self-satisfaction, but rather strive to build relationships of cooperation and community with all other life forms on earth. The roundness we hear in the sound Oh embodies the circle of connection we create when we embrace the world and others in love.

Intention

In the Being of Oh, I will overcome my separateness by affirming love. I will understand the nature of the beloved.

Feeling

Clothed in soft red, I feel the urge to expand beyond my own boundaries. The love of my heart expands with a soft greenish-yellow feeling into the space around me. Imagining myself standing in a circle of people, I round my arms, extending my feeling so that I can touch each individual. I experience a gentle blue tension in my arms as my fingertips meet, and I hold a buoyant circle of love before me.

Movement and Form

Moving from my heart, I extend my arms into a circle, gently and symmetrically rounding them. As is true with all the vowels, I can build the Oh above me, before me, below me, behind me, or even with my legs, and I extend my feeling heart and understanding soul into the shape I create.

Soul Response

I feel the glow of well-being and generosity when I move beyond myself with Oh. The capacity to connect with others opens the doors to love and understanding.

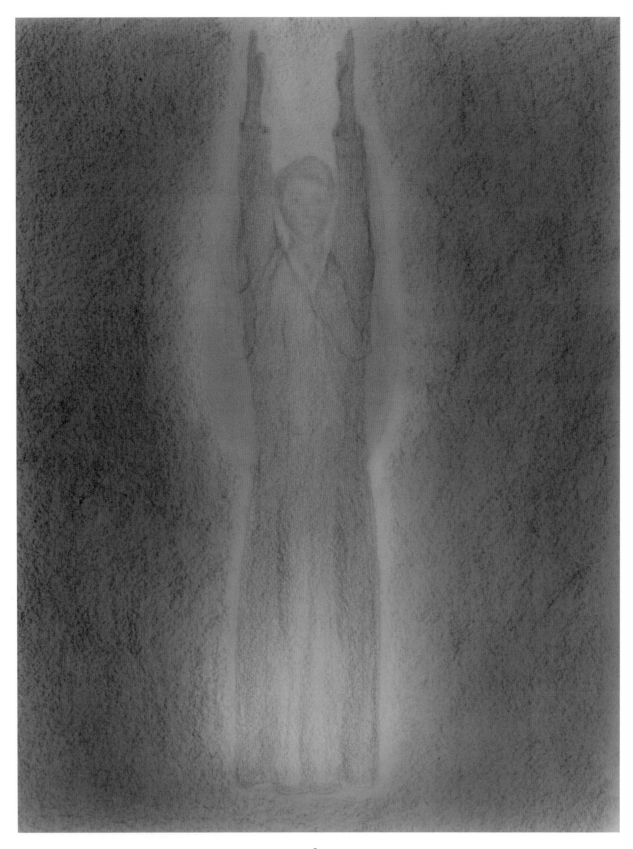

U (OO)

I GATHER THE FRUITS OF MY LIFE AND CREATE A NEW CONNECTION TO THE UNIVERSE AND THE EARTH.

We are born out of the divine womb of the Creator, and will return to it in the fullness of time. Through our experiences in the world of matter, we gain self-awareness, and develop love and understanding for all of creation. Out of our new knowing, we gather our forces and focus our striving, so that we may create the future of the world in a way that is worthy of the source from which it comes. So, too, in the twilight of life each human being sifts through the experiences of life and discovers the gems that lie therein. As we prepare to move beyond the confines of our earthly life and unite ourselves once again with our source, we focus on those things that are essential. We will return to the Creator with the harvest of our lifetime. Both the gold and the dross have served to make us deeper, wiser, and ultimately closer to God.

OO also gives us the strength to stand firmly on the earth. OO is the power that grounds us both on the earth and in eternity.

Intention
I will focus my energy and intention to find the Being of OO.

Feeling
I feel myself rooted in my body, right into the core of my bones, clothed in blue. I feel the strength that has been given to me through the long parallel bones of my arms and legs. I feel quiet and secure. I feel the yellow light of spirit around me and the gesture I create with my arms and legs flows radiantly outward. A gentle lilac tension in my arms holds them close together. If I direct my OO upwards, I connect myself with the heavens; If I direct it downwards, I offer the force of my will to the earth.

Movement and Form
I draw my two arms together, side by side and close to each other. Holding them parallel, I can move them upwards, downwards, or forwards, allowing my forces to stream outwards through them into space

Soul Response
I feel the strength of focus and intention. I am rooted both in heaven and on earth.

HALLELUIAH

The sacred word "Halleluiah" was the first full word that Rudolf Steiner taught in Eurythmy. Rather than teaching it exactly as it is spelled, he showed that it can be expanded by doing many more "L's" than are customarily used. Drawing from he wisdom of the sounds as described in this book, we can understand that this word can be used to create a blessing for oneself and the space one is standing in.

This sequence of meditative pictures was given by Rudolf Steiner to Ilona Schubert, one of the first Eurythmy students.

I begin with my hands crossed in front of my heart, and then open with a "H." My arms are then opened into an Ah above me, and I lower them downwards, maintaining the Ah-angle in a gesture of openness.

I then being a series of seven L's, imagining myself to be standing in front of a pool of crystal-clear water, with which I will cleanse my entire self. The first L is small and low, as I feel my feet. Each subsequent L is larger, until the 7th moves the entire space around me.

I then quietly cross my arms in front of me in the E. I momentarily experience that there are other dimensions of experience I can grow into. Three more L's follow, marking my growth in more subtle, spiritual dimensions.

With the U (oo), I draw my arms together below me, and then raise them to the heights above.

In I (ee), I reach to the stars with my left (selfless) hand, and drop my right hand towards the core of the earth.

I then open both arms in A(ah) towards the heights of heaven above me.

I conclude with the in-breathing H, folding my arms in front of my heart.

A movement meditation:

HALLELUIAH

H	*I open myself to the spirit*
A (ah)	*I let the light of the spirit flow through me*
L	*I cleanse my feet*
L	*I cleanse my knees*
L	*I cleanse my lower body*
L	*I cleanse my feeling (heart)*
L	*I cleanse my speaking (throat)*
L	*I cleanse my thinking (forehead)*
L	*I cleanse my whole self*
E (ā)	*I stand at the threshold to the Spiritual World*
L	*I cleanse spirit-self (imagination)*
L	*I cleanse life-spirit (inspiration)*
L	*I cleanse spirit-man (intuition)*
U (oo)	*I gather my forces and lead them to the spirit*
I (ē)	*From the spirit I receive my ego*
A (ah)	*And that, too, I offer up to God*
H	*And the breath of the spirit returns me to myself*

ABOUT THE AUTHOR

Cynthia Hoven lives in Northern California, where she and her husband celebrate life through Eurythmy and Biodynamic Gardening. Her greatest joy is teaching Eurythmy in public, workshop, private or therapeutic settings. She also gives workshops on the new Cosmology and our relationship to the planets and constellations. Cynthia is also passionately involved in supporting the emergence of new paradigms that will help humanity develop a healthy, thriving and sustainable future on the planet. She will work to spread consciousness and connections wherever she goes.

ABOUT EURYTHMY ALIVE AND ONLINE

Cynthia offers live classes and private sessions in the United States and around the world, including China. Her newest project, eurythmyonline.com, offers over 50 video recordings teaching basic eurythmy movements to enable people to develop eurythmy as a personal movement practice.
In 2014 she also launched her newest project, eurythmyonline.com, a website containing over 50 video recordings teaching basic Eurythmy warm-up exercises, rod exercises, spatial movements, vowels, consonants and soul exercises. It includes free lessons, as well as single lessons, modules and a full basic curriculum. Each lesson includes a video recording, a downloadable pdf, and an opportunity to write and reflect on the practices. Users are instructed to *watch the video, internalize the lessons, and then turn off the video and move in silence.*
Eurythmyonline.com is a gift to the world, to create an opportunities for people around the world to meet it, to experience how it can deepen their spiritual path and understanding, offer forces of health and harmony, and help them open their artistic sensitivities.
Contact Cynthia at info@eurythmyonline.com.

ABOUT THE ILLUSTRATOR
Renée Parks studied art at the University of Michigan, where she earned her BFA in ceramics through doing large-scale sculptures in clay. She is currently a Waldorf class teacher working in Alaska.

Printed in Great Britain
by Amazon